IMAGES OF ENGLAND

Ecclesfield, Grenoside, High Green and Chapeltown

Two moulders, Albert Gibson (left) and Horace Wing (right), tapping the cupola in the light castings foundry at Newton Chambers' Thorncliffe Ironworks. George Sheldon, who worked as a moulder at Thorncliffe from 1936 to 1972, recalls that each operative in the foundry was recognised by the title of his job; there was the mill man who prepared the sand, the cupola tenter who prepared the metal, the fettler who cleaned the casting of its flash and, of course, the moulders, who might include green sand, dry sand, loam, machine or tank plate moulders. Every man or team was expected to draw on personal skills and experience, and improvisation was the order of the day. Nevertheless things sometimes went wrong and men worked all day only to produce a 'waster' for which they were not paid. In spite of hardships, son followed father and grandfather in the craft, many putting in over fifty years of labour and not retiring until their seventies.

IMAGES OF ENGLAND

Ecclesfield, Grenoside, High Green and Chapeltown

Joan and Mel Jones

NONSUCH

A drawing of Ecclesfield church from the south-east by Mrs Juliana Horatia Ewing (1841–1885). Mrs Ewing was the second of ten children of Revd Dr Alfred and Mrs Margaret Gatty. Dr Gatty was vicar of Ecclesfield from 1839 to 1903. Mrs Ewing had a world-wide reputation as a writer of children's stories.

First published 1994
This new pocket edition 2005
Images unchanged from first edition

Nonsuch Publishing Limited
The Mill, Brimscombe Port,
Stroud, Gloucestershire, GL5 2QG
www.nonsuch-publishing.com

British Library Cataloguing in Publication Data.
A catalogue record for this book is available from the British Library.

ISBN 1-84588-123-0

Typesetting and origination by Nonsuch Publishing Limited.
Printed in Great Britain by Oaklands Book Services Limited.

Contents

Introduction

To the casual visitor, the northern suburbs of the present-day Sheffield Metropolitan District are indistinguishable from the outer residential districts of other large urban areas throughout the country. They contain extensive areas of ordinary semi-detached and detached houses and bungalows, largely of red brick with tile roofs, with the occasional high-rise block, intermingled with woods, patches of farmland, parks and playing fields. Additionally there are several modern industrial complexes, with the whole cut through by a number of important roads containing ribbons of retail shops. However, further exploration would reveal that embedded within this suburban sprawl are what were once the four separate village communities of Ecclesfield, Grenoside, High Green and Chapeltown. Together with a number of smaller settlements – such as Charlton Brook, Butterthwaite, Whitley, Bracken Hill and Warren – these once had their own individual identities and characters. Even today these old settlement cores are easily recognised by their building materials – local sandstone and slate.

All of these settlements were once part of the ancient ecclesiastical parish of Ecclesfield. The parish, before its break up into a number of smaller ecclesiastical districts in the nineteenth century, including ones at Grenoside, High Green and Chapeltown, was one of the largest in England, covering nearly 50,000 acres or 78 square miles. This extensive parish was served by the parish church of St Mary's, together with chapels of ease at Bradfield (now St Nicholas' parish church) and Chapeltown (in the Middle Ages, Chapeltown was simply called Chappell, after the chapel there).

The area covered by Ecclesfield, Grenoside, High Green and Chapeltown has relied since time immemorial on the exploitation of the physical resources within its boundaries: the land, woods, stone, coal, iron and the power generated from its small streams and brooks. These gave rise at an early date not only to farming, quarrying, coal and ironstone mining and woodland crafts but also to a tradition of iron production, light metal trades and later to foundry work, engineering and coke and chemicals production. Eventually it was coal mining, foundry products, engineering and chemicals production, together with the inexorable growth of Sheffield and the suburbanisation of its population, that changed the landscape of the area and transformed the once separate villages and hamlets into the interlocking, cosmopolitan residential communities of today.

Before suburbanisation, Ecclesfield was a stone-built village, the original centre of which – called the Town End or Top End – huddled below the parish church and priory, along Church Street, St Mary's Lane, Townend Road and Stocks Hill. Here were a number of inns and taverns and the village stocks. It was probably here that the bull and bear baiting took place that Dr Gatty (see pages 36 and 37), in 1839, referred to as having survived within living memory. The village stretched beyond this core along the present High Street (formerly called

The Wallet), where there was a small green, and along Dog Leg Lane (now Mill Lane) to the common. Behind the village, to the west of the church, is a small stream that flows eastwards and eventually joins Blackburn Brook on the common. This small insignificant brook powered up to six mills, producing at one time or another flour, paper, cotton, scythes and forks. Beyond the village originally lay an open field system and although the open strips were to continue in existence until the late nineteenth century, local farmers were cultivating their strips privately for at least 150 years before that time. Villagers not only cultivated the land and kept livestock but often had a second occupation as well. In the seventeenth and eighteenth century, the most important of these was nailmaking, which was replaced by hand file-cutting in the nineteenth century, which in turn disappeared in the face of competition from machine-made files. Nailmaking was a domestic industry carried on in a nailmaking smithy, many of which were converted into file-making workshops. A small number of these still survive in the village.

Grenoside is the most westerly of the four main settlements and the highest above sea level: the highest part of village is over 800 feet and Greno Wood to the north of the village rises to over 1,000 feet. Until comparatively recently the village was smaller than the other three communities, being described in the mid-nineteenth century as a 'considerable hamlet'. It did not have its own church until 1887 and did not become a separate parish until 1911. Besides farming, employment was traditionally found in quarries, working the Grenoside Sandstone, in the woods (basket making and clog-sole making were local specialities in the nineteenth century) and in the light metal trades such as nailmaking, cutlery manufacture and file-cutting. The area is also famous as the birthplace of and location for the first foundry and steel furnace of the Walker brothers, who later gained fame for their cannons and other heavy castings at their works at Masbrough.

High Green, as the name suggests, began life as a straggling hamlet around a green and remained largely agricultural until the establishment of Thorncliffe Ironworks at the end of the eighteenth century. Together with neighbouring Mortomley it then expanded steadily as an industrial village, to house the workers from the nearby collieries and ironworks, and outgrew both Grenoside and Ecclesfield. It became a separate ecclesiastical district in 1872 with the construction of St Saviour's parish church, built in memory of Parkin Jeffcock, whose mother was a member of a well known High Green family. He lost his life during an heroic rescue attempt at the Oaks Colliery disaster at Barnsley in 1866.

Before industrialisation in the nineteenth century, Chapeltown was a hamlet that had developed around the crossroads where the Sheffield to Barnsley road crossed the Rotherham to Wortley road and where a number of inns and small businesses were located. To the south of the hamlet was a small open field system. The hamlet was also beside Blackburn Brook which powered a corn mill near Cowley Manor and, from the late sixteenth century, the Chapel Furnace next to White Lane to the north of the settlement. This blast furnace was powered by charcoal from the surrounding woods until about 1780; after that date, until about 1860, it operated as a coke-fuelled furnace and the tenants had associated coal and ironstone pits.

However, by the end of the eighteenth century, Chapel Furnace was rivalled by a new industrial development less than a mile further up the Blackburn valley. This would overshadow much of the economic activity in the immediate vicinity and would provide employment not only for the population in Chapeltown and High Green, but also in Ecclesfield and Grenoside. This new development was the Thorncliffe Ironworks of Newton Chambers. The first lease of land from Earl Fitzwilliam of nearby Wentworth Woodhouse was in 1793. A small staff of about a dozen at the beginning of 1794, grew to about 300 in 1800 and nearly 8,000 a century later. The company mined its own ironstone around the works until 1880 and its own coal until the creation of the National Coal Board in 1947. At first the firm manufactured small cast iron goods, but by 1815 was also producing heavy castings and beginning to specialise in gas lighting plant and later gasworks plant. From 1935 the firm also produced excavators and in 1958 bought out Ransome and Rapiers of Ipswich, thereby doubling the firm's excavator production capacity. During the Second World War 1,160 Churchill tanks were made in the excavator factory.

By-products of the coke-making process for the blast furnaces at Thorncliffe, were gases, tars and oils. By the beginning of the 1890s, a germicidal disinfectant had been developed from the oils and in 1893 this was patented as Izal. The product was soon available not only in liquid form, but also as powder, soap, cream and ointment. To this was also added the famous Izal medicated toilet paper. The Chemicals Division eventually became the most profitable part of the firm.

Newton Chambers was taken over by Central & Sheerwood in 1973, subsequently completely re-organised and the most valuable parts sold off. The site of the Thorncliffe Works is now a modern industrial estate, the Izal factory site is a small housing estate and the collieries and coke ovens in the surrounding countryside have completely disappeared.

The tradition and expertise assembled in the area during the rise of Newton Chambers into an industrial giant must have been responsible to some degree for the creation of other small foundry, steel and engineering enterprises in the area. For example, on Ecclesfield Common Green's Foundry (later Moorwood Vulcan) was located; Nether Lane, Ecclesfield was the site of the Hall & Pickles 'Hydra Works'; Charlton Brook was the home of Charlton Ironworks; and Chapeltown was the location of Greenside Foundry and Parramore's Foundry.

Following the highly successful Chapeltown and High Green, published in 1996, this further selection of photographs, extended to cover the neighbouring communities of Ecclesfield and Grenoside, has been chosen not only from the extensive collection of the Chapeltown & High Green Archive, but also from local personal collections and private family albums. Many of the photographs have not previously been published. They constitute a comprehensive pictorial record of the four communities, mainly during the 100 years from about 1875, a period of significant economic and social change. They celebrate people, places, the working environment and leisure time activities and will be of lasting interest to long established residents and relative newcomers alike.

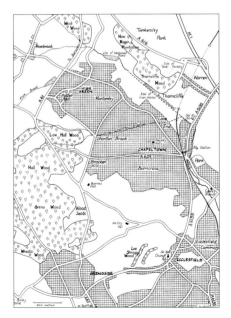

One

Perambulation around Ecclesfield Parish

This section takes the reader on an extensive tour of Ecclesfield parish. Starting in Ecclesfield village, the reader is transported in an anti-clockwise direction to Whitley, Grenoside (with a short excursion to Wharncliffe), Barnes Hall, High Green (with a detour to Westwood), Mortomley, Thorncliffe, Chapeltown, Warren, Burncross, Bracken Hill and back to Ecclesfield village. Almost all of the photographs are from a time when the larger settlements had their own identity, before coalescing with their neighbours or becoming suburbanised.

St Mary's parish church, Ecclesfield. This was the ancient 'mother church' of the once extensive Ecclesfield parish, which, before its dismemberment in the nineteenth century, was one of the largest parishes in England. The ancient parish was gradually reduced in size, first by its separation from Bradfield, which for all intents and purposes had been a distinct parish with its own church from as early as the mid-twelfth century, and then by the creation of new parishes at Wadsley, Oughtibridge, Chapeltown, High Green and Grenoside. The name Ecclesfield is Anglo-Saxon and means a stretch of countryside cleared of woodland (field) with a Celtic church (Eccles). It is generally believed that Ecclesfield was the religious centre of a large Celtic estate, which included the area covered by modern Sheffield and which, by the Middle Ages, had become known as Hallamshire. Saxon and early medieval churches serving areas later sub-divided into independent parishes were called 'minster churches' and significantly St Mary's church has been known for hundreds of years as the 'minster of the moors'. A church has stood on the site since at least the early twelfth century but the present church is largely the result of rebuilding at the end of the fifteenth century in the Perpendicular Style. Important internal changes took place in the nineteenth century.

Right: Ecclesfield Priory, the oldest residential building in Ecclesfield village. It was built next to the parish church to accommodate the monks of the Benedictine Abbey of St Wandrille in Normandy, who had been granted the church and other land in the parish by Richard de Lovetot, Lord of Hallamshire, in the twelfth century. The first mention of the priory was in 1273. In the late fourteenth century the Benedictines were dispossessed and the priory and their possessions in Ecclesfield were given to the Carthusian priory of St Anne at Coventry. After the Dissolution of the Monasteries in the late 1530s, the priory again became the property of the lord of the manor and it was converted into a dwelling house.

Below: Ecclesfield Hall, an extension to the converted priory, was built in 1736 and was the home of a gentleman tenant or farmer at various periods.

The Old Hall, Ecclesfield.

A view of Priory Road (formerly Burying Lane), Ecclesfield, looking south-east towards Church Street. On the right is the Gatty Memorial Hall built in 1904 by public subscription in tribute to the memory of Revd Dr Alfred Gatty. On the left is the church lychgate erected in 1904 to the memory of Henry John Hawthorn, a local and much-respected doctor.

Church Street (formerly Church Lane), Ecclesfield in the early 1900s, looking north-east. Immediately beyond the churchyard wall, this street, consisting mostly of solid sandstone buildings, must have always been a main thoroughfare through the village. Note the early double-decker bus.

St Mary's Lane, Ecclesfield, looking north towards the parish church. The elevated position of the church is clearly visible. The part of St Mary's Lane at the bottom of the dip has been filled in on more than one occasion in order to ease the gradient.

Stocks Hill, an important open space in the centre of the village, with the Feoffees Hall in the centre background, in 1906. The Feoffees Hall was built in the 1730s as a workhouse. From 1854 to 1894 it was used as a school and from 1895 until 1930 for parish council meetings. It was demolished in 1968.

High Street, Ecclesfield. Until the nineteenth century this street was known as Town Street or The Wallet. The right-hand (western) side of the street occupies the former narrow village green.

Nurses' Home, Cross Hill, Ecclesfield (on the right). The building was erected in 1901 in tribute to Thomas William Jeffcock JP, a mining engineer who died in 1900. It originally accommodated two nurses who gave their services freely to the sick.

The Cross, Ecclesfield, looking north towards the Common. The wooded hillside in the background is Smithy Wood.

Cinema House, Ecclesfield Common. Built in 1920, this stood on what is now the car park of the Arundel public house. The entrance was flanked by two shops, one of which was the usual sweet and chocolate shop which remained open until late in the evening to serve the cinema-goers. The building was closed and demolished in the early 1970s.

The hamlet of Butterthwaite. The name, which is of Old Norse origin, means 'woodland clearing with rich pasture'. It was for a long period not only a farming community but also a centre of manufacturing. There was a water-powered mill and various workshops, one of the specialities being gimlet-making.

Whitley Hall. The oldest part of the Hall was built in 1584, with a later wing added in 1683. From Elizabethan times until the late eighteenth century it was the residence of the Shircliffes, an important land-owning family. There was once a water-powered scythe-making mill on the site. It is now a hotel and restaurant.

Penistone Road (now the A61) in Grenoside, looking north, just south of the junction with Blacksmith Lane. This road was turnpiked in 1822. On the extreme left is a wheelwright's house and yard, the latter being used by Heward's, funeral directors, until recently. The outbuildings of Nether House Farm (now demolished) are on the extreme right.

Norfolk Arms on the A61, Grenoside, at the junction of Norfolk Hill and Whitley Lane. This is one of a number of public houses in south-west Yorkshire called the Norfolk Arms, indicating that it stood on land owned by Sheffield's principal landowner – the Duke of Norfolk.

St Mark's church, Grenoside. This church was built on part of Ecclesfield parish glebe land and the foundation stone was laid by the Countess of Wharncliffe in 1884. The first curate-in-charge was the Revd John Evelyn Stacye.

The Stacye Memorial, Grenoside. Following the death of Revd Stacye in 1905, the congregation elected to build a purpose-built vicarage as a memorial. It was built opposite the church, on the site of a former quarry. It was built in a 'cottage-cum-villa' style with decorative wall tiling, bay and corbelled windows and a square battlemented tower. It ceased to be a vicarage in the 1980s.

GRENOSIDE PRIMITIVE METHODIST NEW CHAPEL.

Primitive Methodist chapel on Main Street, Grenoside. Now converted to a private house, this chapel was opened in 1904 to replace an earlier chapel built in 1857. It became surplus to requirements in the 1960s, when the congregation joined in services with the Methodist chapel on Norfolk Hill.

Main Street, Grenoside, looking towards the Old Red Lion, in the early 1900s.

Wharncliffe Crags, a favourite place of recreation for generations of local people. The Crags form a magnificent sandstone edge running for more than three kilometres at the western edge of Wharncliffe Chase. They were used as one of the earliest training grounds for the sport of rock climbing.

Barnes Hall, built by William Smith, formerly of Cowley Manor, after he had purchased the Barnes Hall estate in 1823. The old Barnes Hall, of fourteenth-century date, was demolished to make way for the new one. The Smiths continued to live at Barnes Hall until the 1950s.

Potter Hill, formerly Chapel Lane, at High Green, before twentieth-century housing developments.

Stoneygate Primitive Methodist chapel, High Green. The foundation stones were laid in February 1877. A number of local families were associated with the chapel for over a hundred years, including the Ashtons, Bassinders, Bostwicks, Dransfields, Lockwoods and Vickers'. It was demolished in the late 1980s.

Westwood Rows in the 1960s, shortly before they were demolished and the area landscaped. The rows were built to accommodate non-union labour during the mining dispute involving employees in the collieries of Newton Chambers and Co. at Tankersley and Thorncliffe that lasted for seventeen months, from March 1869 to August 1870. Altogether 850 men and boys were 'locked out' of the pits because they would not agree to a reduction in wages and insisted on union representation. On 21 January 1870 a riot took place in and about the Rows. At seven o'clock in the morning a crowd, variously estimated at between 300 and 1,500 men, some 'armed with pistols, some with bludgeons, the heads of which bristled with spikes, some with picks' according to the *Sheffield and Rotherham Independent*, simultaneously attacked the backs and fronts of the cottages. The cottages were defended by a force of ten policemen who were quickly overwhelmed, though not before despatching a messenger to Barnsley for reinforcements. In the ensuing mayhem windows were smashed, doors and furniture demolished, houses looted and an unsuccessful attempt made to set fire to the houses by burning clothing, bedclothes and broken furniture. Eventually the alarm was raised by blowing the buzzer at Tankersley Colliery which apparently caused the attackers to disperse. Police reinforcements set about the mob with their cutlasses as they scattered. Twenty-three men were sent for trial at York assizes.

Westwood Bottom, an altogether quieter part of the Westwood area, in deep mid-winter.

Mortomley Hill, looking east, with The Old Cart & Horses on the left. In the first quarter of the twentieth century the space in the foreground was used as the venue for the annual Whit Sing for the High Green Sunday schools before moving on to the Ten Acre.

Thorncliffe Works in 1915, looking north-east across the Blackburn Brook valley. Dominating the scene are the two blast furnaces built in 1873-74 to replace those originally built in 1795–96. In the background is Thorncliffe Wood (right) and Newbiggin Plantation (left), the latter was planted over early coal and ironstone pits.

Thorncliffe Rows. These were built for Newton Chambers in the 1860s to house blackleg miners during the disputes of 1866 and 1869–70. The cottages were demolished in the late 1960s.

The Bridge Inn, Lane End. The inn ceased trading in 1956 and was demolished around 1960.

Housley Park, Chapeltown in the early years of the twentieth century. This rural scene was no more than half a mile from Thorncliffe Ironworks. On the right is St John's church, consecrated in 1860, and in the centre is Mount Pleasant Methodist church dating from 1866.

Chapeltown vicarage, standing in the shadow of St John's church. The building has recently been converted into a set of parish rooms.

Whitefields, Chapeltown, later to become Sussex Road. This led to the former Midland Railway station.

The Yorkshire Penny Bank, at the junction of Greenside (now Burncross Road) and Lound Side, Chapeltown. The bank was built around 1900 with the manager's house above it. Behind, to the left, is the Midland Hotel, now The Escape.

Chapeltown crossroads in the days of light traffic! On the right is the Waggon & Horses, now Scandals. In the centre is the Midland Railway bridge which was built in 1891. On the left are two lock-up shops and on the extreme left, The Cosy Café.

Tennis courts and bowling green behind the Newton Hall (the building on the extreme left).
The tall building in the centre background is the Midland Bank on Station Road, built in
1912. To the left of the Midland Bank is the Midland Railway bridge, with the chimneys of
Smith Street protruding above it.

A BIT OF OLD CHAPELTOWN (Dr. Snadden's House)

Dr Snadden's house, Chapeltown, built in an area now covered by the railway embankment.
When the house was demolished in the 1890s Dr Snadden moved to Greenhead House. Dr
Snadden's house is believed to have been built by two bachelor brothers called Falding. It was
home to a succession of local doctors.

Station Road, Chapeltown, c. 1900. On the right is the Chapeltown Co-op, which at that time contained grocery, drapery, boot and shoe and butchering departments. The white-aproned figure standing beside his shop on the far left is Wilf 'Chinny' Cooper, hairdresser and general store keeper.

Wilf 'Chinny' Cooper's shop. In addition to a quick shave and haircut, goods such as working boots, leather laces, metal 'snap' tins and water bottles were sold, to mention but a few. You name it and Chinny sold it, as is clearly illustrated.

Left: Demolition of the aerial ropeway across White Lane. This ropeway was developed in the late 1920s to transport coal from Rockingham Colliery and Thorncliffe to Smithywood coking plant. It was used until the mid-1960s.

Below: Warren Lane, looking towards the Barnsley road (the A6135) in the early 1900s. By this time the southern side of the road had become an industrial village with most of the working population employed at Newton Chambers' Thorncliffe Works.

Above: Greenside, Chapeltown, looking towards Chapeltown crossroads in the early 1900s. The Midland Railway bridge can be seen in the distance. The shop next to which the man is leaning, belonged to Edward Milns who ran a combined drapery and grocery business.

Below: Housley Villas, Burncross – superior Edwardian residences.

Horsley Villas, Chapeltown.

Hunshelf View, Burncross, a solid terrace of four dwellings in brick and stone, built in the early 1900s.

Burncross House, now demolished, and its cottage garden.

Bracken Hill Camp was originally designed to house homeless Sheffielders in the Second World War. It was never used for that purpose but instead housed British troops and then Dutch evacuees. A private housing estate now occupies the site.

The New Inn, Bracken Hill, and adjoining cottages in the early 1900s. The New Inn became a public house in about 1863 and closed in 1913. Arthur Marsden, the landlord, his wife Myra, and their son, Charlie, are standing near the pub doorway.

Chapeltown Road (formerly Coit Lane), Ecclesfield, looking towards Ecclesfield village (right) and Common (left), c. 1900. Note that the road is not 'metalled' and must have been a mudbath at certain times of the year. Skirt lengths were quite unsuitable when pushing a pram. The road was one of the earliest turnpikes in the Sheffield area (running between Sheffield, Barnsley and Wakefield) and dates from 1758. From 1876 it was no longer a turnpike road. In the middle distance, at the end of the boundary wall, a toll-booth cottage is visible, at which tolls were gathered for the upkeep of the road. The building on the opposite side of the road from the toll-bar cottage was for a time a public house called The Plough. In the right middle-ground, with its chimney, is a mill that probably began life as a medieval water-powered corn mill. It later became a cotton mill and by 1848 had been converted into a paper mill. The paper mill was destroyed by fire. The mill dam survives behind the present day Working Men's Club and is stocked with coarse fish. In the left background can be seen the cottages on Mill Lane (formerly Dog Leg Lane). In the right background, on its prominent site, is the tower of St Mary's parish church.

Two

People

In the earliest times people were attracted to Ecclesfield, Grenoside, High Green and Chapeltown to farm the land, exploit the woods and quarry stone. From the sixteenth century the ironstone in the area gave rise to iron manufacturing and some steel production. However, it was not until the nineteenth century, with the expansion of the light metal trades in Ecclesfield and Grenoside and the rapid growth of the Thorncliffe Ironworks, that the area began to attract migrants from other regions. The new migrants not only mined coal and ironstone and worked in the metal trades, they came to work in a variety of other capacities, for example as school teachers, domestic servants and shop assistants. As the nineteenth-century demand for labour stabilised during the twentieth century, further expansion of the population was stimulated by planned overspill from Sheffield. In addition, people coming to work in the surrounding region were attracted by middle-priced housing in a convenient location for travel to work by car. The various stimuli to population growth over a long period have given the four communities a rich blend of origins, cultures and enthusiasms. The photographs in this section have been selected to represent the contribution of people from all walks of life to the district's distinctive character in the past.

The christening of Rosemary Scott Smith in the early 1900s. Rosemary is held by her great grandfather, the Revd Alfred Gatty DD, vicar of Ecclesfield from 1839 until his death in 1903. The baby's mother, Beatrice Smith, is to the right of Dr Gatty, with her husband, Francis Smith, standing in the centre. The baby's grandfather, Francis Patrick Smith stands on the far right. Francis Patrick Smith was a landowner, farmer, solicitor and local squire. Alfred Gatty was the quintessential Victorian 'gentleman-parson', who recorded his long incumbency at Ecclesfield in his book *A Life at One Living*. His first wife, Margaret Scott Gatty, daughter of the Revd Alexander John Scott, Lord Nelson's chaplain at Trafalgar, was far better known than her husband. She was an 'exquisite calligraphist', an expert on sundials, a landscape artist, writer on natural history (she was an authority on British seaweeds), but above all a writer for children in which capacity she had a world-wide reputation and readership. Dr and Mrs Gatty also raised a family of eight surviving children of rare talent. Their second daughter, Juliana Horatia (Mrs Ewing) had an even greater literary reputation as a children's writer than her mother. The settings of some of her best stories were inspired by the landscape around Ecclesfield and Grenoside. Two of the Gatty sons were knighted.

The Revd Dr Alfred Gatty is surrounded by members of St Mary's church choir in the early 1890s after a Whit Monday service, outside the vicarage. Back row, from left to right: Fred Robinson, Joe Sansby, Billy Cutts, Billy Hemmingfield, David Parker, Joe Unwin, Harry Turton. Second row: David Parker Snr (organist), Amos Parker, Arthur Gledhill, Mr Smith (Dr Gatty's gardener), Reg Harper, Archie Harper (the main soloist), Ben Cutts, Alfred Stringer, Albert Smith, Alf Higgins, Harry Gregory, Mr Tom Bramheld (choirmaster). Third row: Alf Flather, Ernest Flather, Fred Whitham, Ernest Whitham, Horace Burked, Percy Stringer, Arthur Sorsby, Harry Flather. Fourth row: Walter Hague, Reg Howson, Ernest Cutts, Revd Dr Alfred Gatty, Myers Stevenson or Maurice Kime, Albert Bradshaw. Front row: Len Flather, Harry Flather, Bernard Higgins, Willie Loxley, Billy Flather, Math Jepson. In *A Life at One Living*, Dr Gatty wrote 'our choir consists of volunteers, that is, they are not paid for their services; but they give a concert every year in the Infant School, which is always well attended; and they share amongst themselves the profits that arise from the sale of sittings. They also have a trip to the sea, or elsewhere, with a dinner, for which the offertories pay.'

Henry and Sarah Greaves celebrate their wedding anniversary in 1906, on Cross Hill, Ecclesfield. Among those standing are: Sally Greaves, Fred Greaves, Benjamin Greaves and Walter Greaves. Sitting on the front row are: Leonard Greaves, Phoebe Greaves, John Willoughby Greaves, Roland Frederick Greaves, -?-, Sally Greaves, Harry Martin -?-.

A late Victorian seaside studio portrait. Benjamin Greaves of Cross Hill, Ecclesfield, with his wife Florence (both seated) and their son, Roland, had this portrait taken in a studio at Blackpool.

Dressed in the fashion of the day are John Willoughby Greaves (left), born 1903, and Roland Frederick Greaves (right), born 1898. Their parents were Benjamin and Florence Greaves. Both John and Roland became farmers at Rainstorth Farm, Ecclesfield.

An Ecclesfield football team, possibly from Green's Foundry, in the 1950s. Back row, from left to right: Sydney Gillot, P.C. Lee, Clifford Holdon, Peter Anson, Alan Kay, Clarence Belcher, George Beever, Barry Tyrell, Ken Senior, Bill Timms, Frank Turner, -?-. Front row: -?-, ? Smith, ? Whitham, Walter Cattel, Gordon Guest, Peter Lynch or Terry Mellor, -?-.

Another Ecclesfield football team. Back row, from left to right: -?-, B. Hemingfield, Harold Goodison, -?-, -?-, Russell Heely, Ken Boulding, D. Tingle, H. Crossland, -?-. Front row: Eric Gregory, B. Ridge, Ron Hall, Alan Sharpe, -?-, J. Gandy.

Memorial to Sir Richard Scott of Barnes Hall in St Mary's church, Ecclesfield. He died in Ireland in July, 1638, at the age of 55. At the time he was acting as one of the Council to Thomas Wentworth, the Earl of Strafford who was Commander-in-Chief there. Scott had led an adventurous life, once falling into the hands of the Spanish Inquisition. This fine monument, made of alabaster, cost £120. According to Gatty, in *A Life at One Living*, the original contract, of which he had seen a copy, stated that an order was given for the 'best matterialls' and 'Sir Richard Scott, knight, is to be maide resting on one side, with his hand under his head, on a cushion and matt, with helme also under his head; all in compleat armour; his sworde girt to his side, his spurrs on his heels, and craft of honour at his feet. All this, and every part in one entyre whole stone of the purest and best white alabaster ... every part to be as strongly built, sett, and finished ... in the best matterialls aforesaide; and cheiffest workmannshipp, with God's helpe at or before Whitsuntide next in the yeare 1640 in the parish church of Ecclesfield.' The monument was shipped from London to Hull and then by land carriage to Bawtry and it was finally brought to Ecclesfield at the expense of Mr Housley Freeman of Housley Hall, Chapeltown.

Ecclesfield born, Mr and Mrs Willoughby Hartley outside their cottage, now demolished, near the bottom of Yew Lane. Here they brought up ten children, five boys and five girls. The youngest son became a regular soldier but the other four were miners, like their father, at Barley Hall pit. During the miners' strike in 1926 two of the brothers, Dick and Joe, who were members of Ecclesfield Silver Prize Band, went away with a few other players for a week at a time. They slept rough and tramped as far as Huddersfield playing to crowds who gathered around them and gave money.

Right: Dr Henry John Hawthorn of Ecclesfield. At the time of the 1871 census Dr Hawthorn was a 33 year-old General Practitioner living on Church Lane with two unmarried sisters, Anne Hawthorn (aged 31) and Susannah Hawthorn (aged 24). James King, a 'student of Glasgow University', was his assistant and lived with them. They were looked after by Sarah Rodgers of High Green and Henrietta Platts from Masbrough, both domestic servants. Dr Hawthorn lived and worked in Ecclesfield for the rest of his life. The lychgate of St Mary's church was erected in his honour.

Below: Mr Curdew Smith of Townend Road, Ecclesfield, celebrating his 100th birthday with his grand-daughter, June. Mr Smith had worked at Newton Chambers and was visited on his birthday by Sir Harold West who gave him a pipe and two months' supply of his favourite tobacco.

Left: George Albert French of Grenoside, born 1886 was the second son of Frederick William and Martha French. His father had a smithy and cottage on Blacksmith Lane. He, too, trained as a blacksmith but later worked at Newton Chambers.

Below: The wedding of Annie Eke and Charles Womersley on 13 June 1912, at St Mark's, Grenoside. The bride wore a silk dress. Two of the six bridesmaids were Maggie and Mary Womersley. Cecil Womersley was best man.

Opposite above: Mr and Mrs Adams (seated, fourth and fifth from left), were the new Master and Matron at Grenoside Poor Law Institution in September 1930.

Right: Mr and Mrs George Senior, bakers of Lump Lane, Grenoside, with their son Harry. The Seniors started their bakery after George Senior lost the sight of an eye in a mining accident at Thorpe pit. They decided to set up a bakery in their home at 7 Lump Lane in 1920. Mrs Senior, with the help of her daughter, Nelly, made pikelets, oatcakes and teacakes. George went round the district on foot, selling their baking from a basket. The front room of the house was turned into a shop and a small bakehouse was built onto the back. The business expanded and in 1928 they moved to a three acre site close by. Eventually a horse-drawn van was bought for deliveries and later a motorised vehicle. For many years their son, Denis, drove the van, as did Lawrence Fleetwood. They produced bread and confectionery of all types. They supplied confectionery to Walsh's of Sheffield and bread to Cockayne's in addition to four shops of their own (in Chapeltown, Crosspool, Parkhead and Bradway) and several market stalls. The business ceased trading in 1991.

Ada Gibson (née Brownhill), born 1869, of Barnes Green Farm, is on the left, with her two eldest children, Willis and Mary. On the right is her sister, Sarah Redfern, who was born in 1867, of Bracken Hill, with her two sons, Brownhill and Stephen.

Some members of Stoneygate Methodist chapel, High Green. Back row, from left to right: Jim Dransfield, Ed Boswell, Tom Bassinder, Harold Vickers, Jack Lockwood, Joe Ashton. Front row: Elijah Wragg, Frank Bassinder, -?-, Fred Vickers.

Right: Joe and Lottie Ashton, née Walton, and their daughter, Doreen. Lottie met Joe while enjoying Sunday tea at a friend's house when he was preaching at Station Road Methodist chapel. So began a romance that led to their marriage at Burncross chapel in 1909. Joe was successively a Co-op butcher's boy, miner at Wharncliffe Silkstone Colliery at Pilley, and fish and chip shop proprietor in Thompson Hill, High Green.

Below: In the early 1920s, Joe Ashton began a Bible class at Stoneygate Methodist chapel and before long a football team was formed and played in a local league. Back row, from left to right: Joe Ashton, Edward Childs, Doug Dransfield, Jim Davis, Reg Swift, Albert Walker, Percy Turner, Albert Mayo, Doug Armitage, Billy Wroe, Tom Jowitt. Front row: Albert Denton, -?-, Arnold Crossland, Ernest Dunwell, Horace Hawkins.

Above left: Clifford Davis (right) and his brother, Jim Davis, outside their house at 10 New Street, High Green, *c.* 1915. After leaving school Clifford became a miner and then worked for Newton Chambers in charge of a team that erected gasholders in different parts of the country. During the Second World War he joined Sheffield City Police and later worked for the Prudential Insurance Company.

Above right: Fred Sorsby and his wife Rebecca (née Pepper) with their young daughter, Alice, *c.* 1914. Fred was a pattern maker at Parramore's Foundry in Chapeltown. Rebecca's family kept the Travellers Inn on Cowley Hill. Alice married Clifford Davis in February 1935.

Above left: John Hornsby of High Green with his son, Ernest. Both were members of St Saviour's church choir. Because there was no bank in High Green the church school room was used as a distant outpost of the Yorkshire Penny Bank. It was only open on Friday evenings and older members of the community remember taking their savings there where they were entered by Mr Hornsby. Ernest continued to take an interest in music and at one time was musical director of the High Green Operatic Society.

Above right: Mildred Beever, schoolteacher, *c.* 1910. Mildred was the eldest of the six children of George and Blanche Beever of High Green. She attended High Green School (Wortley Road) as a pupil, where her academic abilities were noticed. When she was old enough to leave she was offered the post of pupil teacher at the school. This she accepted and, like many other 13 year olds all over the country, she began the long apprenticeship of learning to be a teacher. The pupil teachers did not go away to college but learned on the job, through experience and night classes. She married Harry Walker of Ecclesfield and they had a son, George. When Harry died at a relatively young age, the young widow returned to teaching at High Green School where she remained until her retirement.

The Jones family of Wortley Road, High Green. Mr Alfred Jones was born in Wales but left as a young man to look for work. After staying with relatives in Manchester he came to High Green where he worked for Newton Chambers as a miner. He married Annie, a local girl, and lived out his life in High Green. Back row, from left to right: Ellis, Ralph, Alvey. Middle row: Alice, Mrs Annie Jones, Alford, Mr Alfred Jones, Annie. Front: Alder and Alfred.

This nicely posed Edwardian portrait is of Charles Albert Falding of Chapeltown. He was the youngest in a family of six, three boys and three girls. Both his parents belonged to well known local families who had lived in the parish for generations. His father's family were blacksmiths and farmers on Cowley Lane, near the crossroads, and the old farmhouse has only recently been demolished. His mother was one of the daughters of Enoch Moore, farmer at Charlton Brook. Charles married Isobel Mangham of Thorpe Hesley and they had three sons Edward, John and David. His eldest brother, Tom, took over Cowley Lane Farm while Charles pursued office work in and around Chapeltown and Sheffield.

Right: Amy Prior of Charlton Brook, pictured during the Second World War when she was working for the National Fire Service. She was a telephonist, call sign E2Q, at Chapeltown fire station which was based in huts behind Chapeltown Picture Palace. Her section leader was Mr Dick Endall.

Below: Some members of the Stutchbury family at Wharncliffe Crags in the 1920s. The Crags have always been a popular venue for a ramble.

Pictured are, from left to right: Mabel Frances Westerman, a pupil teacher at Burncross School, with her sister, Freda, and her mother, Clara Westerman (née Hirst), c. 1897. Mabel married Arnold Warburton, who became secretary to Mr Newton of Newton Chambers. They lived on Burncross Road throughout their married lives.

Right: Arthur Marsden and his wife, Myra, (née Beever) with their son Charles Arthur, *c.* 1906. Arthur kept the New Inn at Bracken Hill. When the public house ceased trading in 1913 it became a shop. Myra worked in the shop until 1963. She died in 1964 at the age of 86.

Below: Elizabeth Chapman and her daughters (from left to right), Elizabeth, Ann and Sarah, in a water-colour painting dated 1858. Elizabeth Chapman (née Champion) married Thomas Chapman, filesmith and landlord of the Acorn Inn at Bracken Hill, in the mid-1830s. They had three sons, William, Matthew and Frederick and the three daughters portrayed here.

Edward Brownhill (born 1837), farmer at Windmill Hill Farm. He took over the running of the farm from his father, George. Edward married Mary Sanderson whose father had a farm on the Wicker in Sheffield. Their two daughters were Sarah and Ada. The house at Windmill Hill Farm was described by Jonathan Eastwood in his *History of the Parish of Ecclesfield* (1862) as a 'substantial old farmhouse'. It was formerly the residence of the Pawson family in the Elizabethan period. It is no longer a working farm.

Brownhill Redfern, born in the mid-1890s, was the eldest son of William and Sarah Redfern. He was a gunner in the First World War and fought in France. He married Olive Hudson of Howbrook and worked for Newton Chambers. He died in 1969.

Evelyn Rodgers (left), Jean Sheldon and Edna Rodgers were Land Army Girls, during the Second World War. Evelyn worked on an arable farm in Worksop and then a dairy farm in Wombwell, where she learned to milk by hand, before becoming a 'rodent operative' in the local area.

Eric Green sitting on the rocking horse belonging to Burncross Primary School in 1935. Molly Dolby is standing beside him.

Bert Almond of Chapeltown (left), was Sheffield Amateur Billiards Champion in 1937. Ernest Almond, his brother (right), was Sheffield Amateur Snooker Champion, also in 1937.

Harold and Emma Lewis and their two sons, Harold and Norman. Harold married Emma Ellison at Mount Pleasant in September 1913. Harold worked at Newton Chambers, becoming the Chief Electrical Engineer in the early 1930s. Some of the family were members of Chapeltown Operatic Society and Emma played the piano in Chapeltown Picture Palace when silent pictures were shown.

Three young men from Chapeltown attired in their holiday clothes, just before the First World War, at Cunningham's holiday camp on the Isle of Man. From left to right: Maurice Senior, Arnie Warburton, Ernest Bellamy.

The wedding photograph of James Greaves and Alice Yeulett, taken in Hobart, Tasmania on 14 April 1887. James was one of nine children of Mary and Benjamin Greaves who had built a house, workshop and smithy at Charlton Clough. James emigrated in 1884 and settled in Hobart with Alice who had left Hampshire in 1883. Trained by his father, James was a skilled cabinet maker and made a good living in Tasmania.

Enoch Moore of Charlton Brook Farm with his wife, Mary, and three of his daughters. For many years Enoch Moore was a member of the Board of Guardians at Wortley Union Workhouse. He died in 1895, aged 78.

Three

Earning a Living

Traditionally, employment in Ecclesfield, Grenoside, High Green and Chapeltown was tied to the land and what it produced – not just farm crops and livestock, but also wood and timber, stone, coal and ironstone. Farming was always an important staple industry and, despite early industrialisation and later suburbanisation, there are still working farms in the area. Above all, though, the four main settlements became widely known for their quarries, collieries, ironstone mines and their metal-based manufacturing industries. Iron was not only the basis of the blacksmith's craft but also that of nailmakers, file-cutters, forkmakers and gimlet makers and contributed to the establishment of small iron foundries and the massive growth of a major ironworks and foundry complex at Thorncliffe. As the populations of the main settlements grew, so the services to meet residents' needs proliferated – grocery shops, drapery shops, inns, taverns and beerhouses, boot and shoe makers, butchers, blacksmiths, postmasters, surgeons, carters, station masters and horse omnibus proprietors, to name but a few.

Traditional farming as practised by the Greaves family at Rainstorth Farm, Ecclesfield in the 1930s. Rainstorth Farm lies on the extreme eastern edge of the ancient parish of Ecclesfield and now has the M1 motorway running close by. The Greaves family, consisting of Roland Greaves and his wife, his parents Benjamin and Florence, and his brother John Willoughby Greaves, took over the farm in 1929. Prior to this they had a small holding (with a few cows) as a second employment and had developed a small milk-round at Cross Hill, Ecclesfield. In a previous generation the Greaves' had run a hand-cut file works at Cross Hill. These scenes show the farm horseman, Sam Eaton, harvesting oats.

Sam Eaton, the Rainstorth Farm horseman, is turning hay in the 1930s on an outlying piece of land in another part of Ecclesfield.

John Willoughby Greaves, outside his poultry shed at Rainstorth Farm in the early 1930s.

Above: Laura Greaves (left) and Nellie Barlow are delivering milk by horse and cart for John Willoughby Greaves of Cross Hill, Ecclesfield. This was some years before the Greaves' moved to Rainstorth Farm. The cart was made by Clarke's of Wortley Road, Thorpe Hesley and cost £52.

Left: Domestic staff at Shire House, Shiregreen. This was the residence of the Dixon family, well known cutlers. In the Victorian and Edwardian period many local girls found employment in domestic service in the local area and further afield. On the left is Anna Mason, parlour maid, originally from Woodhouse. She married Arthur John Parramore, a member of the Ecclesfield handbell ringers. After they married they lived on Church Street, Ecclesfield.

Staff of Henry Greaves' hand file-cutting workshop, St Michael's Works, Cross Hill, Ecclesfield. Henry Greaves stands at the back on the right. The hand cutting of large flat files was exceedingly laborious. The worker sat with his knees on either side of his 'stiddy' (anvil), resting on a stone pillar. Sitting on the stiddy was a slab of lead on which the file was placed when cutting. As the lead was relatively soft it minimised the recoil from the blow of the hammer and also prevented any damage to the cut surface when the file was cut on the reverse side. The file was held in place by a leather strap or stirrup, secured by the filecutter's foot. Using a hammer and chisel, the filecutter rapidly produced a set of parallel ridges of great uniformity and exactness. When the file was to be used on hard surfaces, it was usually cross-cut with a second series of diagonal ridges. A medium file could have as many as 1,000 cuts on each side and 300 on each edge. A skilled worker, working for ten hours, could cut about 20 such files in a day, using a 7lb hammer for the face and a 3lb hammer for the sides. The filecutters' disease was lead poisoning. Where a number of men worked in the same shop, fine particles of lead were everywhere. The lead was constantly being handled when the file was turned and 'snap' was often eaten with unwashed hands. Thus in a variety of ways lead was absorbed into the system. Bending over the files when working and using heavy hammers caused back and wrist complaints. When the blank files were all cut, they were taken to Sheffield every Saturday by Henry Greaves and payment was received. At the beginning of the following week few files were cut and there was much 'laiking' (absenteeism and slow progress with long breaks). This would be followed by a few days of frantic activity to fulfil the order for Saturday.

Brightside and Carbrook Co-operative Stores on High Street, Ecclesfield in the early twentieth century.

Apprentices and staff of Hall & Pickles' Tool Engineering Department, in 1956. Back row, from left to right: John Pickering, Derek Armitage, Derek Crapper, Alan ?, Terry Dronfield, -?-, Brian Timm, Keith Eccles, -?-. Middle row: Brian Clarke, David Crisp, Brian Cooper, Keith Foster, Alan Frisby, Philip Eadon, Bernard Parkin, Mike Whitehouse, Terry Biggins, Albert Lupton, Keith Tollerfield. Front row: David Ridge, Jeff Driver, David Proctor, Raymond Willey, Fred Haslam, Mr J.H. Russell, Mr Murphy, Sam Hartley, -?-, Major Higgins.

Post office, Penistone Road, Grenoside. Charles Womersley and his wife, Sarah, kept the shop and post office in the early 1900s. Their older children delivered the mail and here we see that Cecil and Maggie are ready for their deliveries. Cecil also helped his father with the horses because Mr Womersley carried stone from the local quarries, fetched house coal by the ton from the Thorncliffe Drift, hawked fruit and vegetables and was also a carrier of goods from Sheffield to Grenoside.

Beever's Quarry, Grenoside in 1906. Stone quarrying was a major industry in Grenoside during the late nineteenth and early twentieth centuries, reaching its peak around 1900 when about 150 men and boys were employed. The sandstone quarried was the Grenoside Sandstone. The stone was used for many purposes depending on its grain and density. It was in demand for grindstones, furnace linings, building stone, kerbstones, gate posts and walling stone. Hillsborough Barracks (now a Morrison's superstore) and the GPO in Fitzalan Square, Sheffield, are reputed to be constructed of Grenoside Sandstone. The Beever family operated quarries in an area between Stephen Lane and Main Street.

Arthur Hoyland, gamekeeper for Mr Bingley at Whitley Hall, in the early 1900s. Arthur's main job was vermin control in the fields and woodlands in the Whitley valley. He used to set up a vermin rack, a line between two trees, and hang on it stoats, weasels, rats, magpies and even herons that took trout from the ponds. He and the tenant farmers used to rear pheasants in the woods at Woodend and Blackwood alongside Elliott Lane. The Bingleys also owned Ellerslie Lodge on the Woodhead Moors and Arthur was responsible for the grouse shooting there.

Lottie Walton in service in Bradford. Having a lot of strong hair she always had trouble with hats! Lottie was born at Scholes in a cottage near to Keppel's Column. She had a very deprived childhood, being one of eight children whose mother died in childbirth. She left home when she was thirteen and did not have a home again until she married. She started work at the Children's Hospital scrubbing stone corridors every day and later went into domestic service. She married Joe Ashton in 1909.

Early nineteenth-century view of the Thorncliffe Ironworks of Newton Chambers. In the right foreground two figures on horseback are approaching the two open-topped blast furnaces erected under the supervision of Thomas Chambers, who ran the practical side of the business. In the background, on Furnace Hill, between the works and Thorncliffe Wood (where the mining of coal and ironstone was taking place), the activity illustrated is likely to be the stacking of ironstone and/or coke, ready for barrowing into the furnaces. It was the usual practice for ironstone to be left on the ground for a year or more during which time it weathered (calcined) and became easier to separate from the shale in which it was embedded. The first furnace was completed by the end of April 1795 and had a capacity of 15 tons of metal per week. The second furnace, finished in 1796, had a capacity of 20 tons a week. Behind the left-hand blast furnace stands a steam-engine house whose role it was to provide the cold blast of air for the furnaces. The buildings nearby are casting sheds and other foundry shops. In the early days of the business Thomas Chambers lived in a cottage in the foundry yard, possibly the building on the right-hand edge of the view.

Right: Tapping a blast furnace at Thorncliffe. This blast furnace was built in 1927 (and re-conditioned in 1933) to replace the existing three furnaces, two built in 1873–74 and another in 1913. In full blast, the 1927 furnace could produce 50,000 tons of pig iron a year, and between 1927 and 1942, when pig iron production stopped, it yielded nearly 619,000 tons of pig iron.

Below: The gates for Mauritius Botanical Gardens were cast at Newton Chambers' Thorncliffe Ironworks in 1867.

Churchill tanks are lined up ready for testing outside the Warren Lane works. During the Second World War Newton Chambers produced 1,160 Churchill tanks at the factory on Warren Lane, which had been designed for excavator production. In the background is the aerial ropeway carrying coal from Rockingham Colliery.

Celebrating the 1,000th Churchill tank off the production line. Harold (later Sir Harold) West, managing director, is in the centre, holding his hat and a walking stick.

This Newton Chambers locomotive is pulling a train of empties away from the Midland Railway sidings, to be loaded with various Newton Chambers' products, in about 1930. The locomotive is probably one of the Thorncliffe series, Thorncliffe No. 1 or No. 6. It is near the hand-operated lever points, where the fan-like arrangement of the marshalling yard came together to take the wagons back to the works. The railway line nearest to us led round the back of the offices in a cutting, crossing the Blackburn Brook over the Five Arches to deliver ore and limestone to the blast furnace. In the background is the Boiler Shop and on the other side of the wooden fence is the shed for locomotive repairs. The cylindrical tank hanging vertically within a the framework is the hydraulic accumulator which supplied water under pressure for various hydraulic machines in the Boiler Shop.

Norfolk Chemical Works, 1918. Back row, from left to right: E. Smith, N. Sheldon, D. Utley, L. Hobson, A. Tromans, R. Norman, E. Fullelove, A. Parkin, E. Parkin, ? Marshall, H. Ogden. Third row: F. Norman, L. Woodhead, W. Gregory, M. Galloway, F. Rowland, E. North, H. Westerman, H. Searson, M. Rowley, N. Fenwick, A. North, G. Coggan. Second row: A. Thompson, A. Sylvester, A. Hawks, M. Portman, M. Fox, M. Brown, H. Hutchinson, E. Roberts, B. Ashton, M. Turner, P. Roberts, G. Elliot, F. Rowland, V. Boyes (manager), G. Humberstone. Front row includes: M. Ducker, M. Bellamy, D. Gressy, A.J. Smith (supervisor), E. Curry, L. Littlewood, M. Colton, L. Sellers, A. Littlewood.

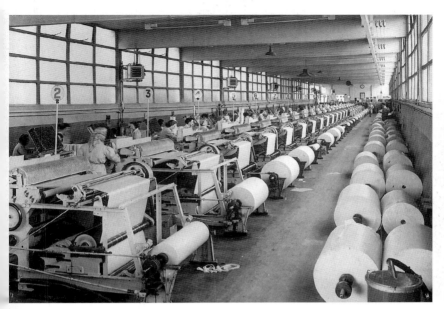

An interior view of the Izal factory at Chapeltown. Work began on this purpose-built factory in 1930 for the reeling and medication of Izal toilet paper. The trade name Izal was registered in 1893. The germicidal oil was a by-product of coal and became world famous in the fight against disease.

The cars used by the sales representatives are lined up outside the headquarters of Newton Chambers at Thorncliffe, in 1934.

Newton Chambers opened their Works College in 1943 in which training was provided for those joining the firm. This group of girls, pictured in January 1950, was trained by Miss Berry (front, centre). Each girl was attached to an office in the morning but attended the college in the afternoon. The standards achieved meant they were the *crème de la crème* of the local office world.

Newton Chambers Engineering Training Centre apprentices, in the 1940s. Left to right: H. Frost, E. Hyde, F. Maskell, E. Watkinson, H. Lee, H. Cooke, S. Barber, R. Waller, T. Ramsden, R. Bristow, B. Young.

Izal factory ladies' football team, in the late 1940s. Back row, from left to right: Jean Burkinshaw, -?-, Dolly Jackman, Martha Thorpe, Mary Harris, ? Woodward. Front row: Doris Lakin, Kath Horne, Nancy ?, Eileen Pinder, Margaret Walker.

Thorncliffe Recreational Association Football Club, 1953-54. Back row, from left to right: R. Southam, B. Hulbert, A. Hood, D. Moore, B. Hall, I. Gentles, T. Fleetwood, G. Blackburn. Front row: B. Midlane, I. Purvis, G. Mappin (captain), D. Pink and T. Mellor.

William Redfern, a farm worker on the Barnes Hall estate, ploughing with shire horses.

Olive Hudson turning the hay at Windmill Hill Farm just before the First World War.

Hay harvest, probably at Burncross (Hill Top) farm. William Redfern stands with the horse and Arnold Warburton holds a child's hand. Mrs Sarah Redfern stands wearing her white apron. Are they having a goose for the harvest supper?

Looking from Greengate Lane towards Hollow Gate in the 1920s. Prior to the building of this road through the rock outcrop, the track had veered off to the left in front of Charlton Brook Farm before emerging again above the Bridge Inn. During this period several new roads were constructed in the area to improve communications and provide work for the unemployed. It is thought that Albert Whittaker, of Charlton Brook and Kenneth Cauwood of Stocks Hill, Ecclesfield are two of the workmen.

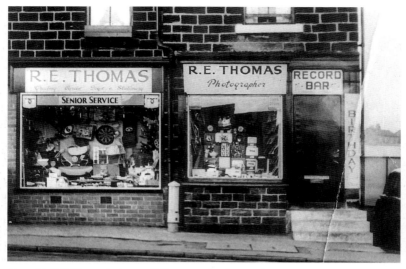

Above: Mr R.E. Thomas's shop at 60 Burncross Road. Ron Thomas was a well-known local photographer and kept these premises for many years. Other items sold included records, stationery and toys. The store was very popular with local children at Christmas when Father Christmas would appear in a grotto there.

Above: Workers at Parramore's Foundry, Chapeltown.

Right: Alex Parramore making the last cast at Parramore's Foundry, Chapeltown, on 5 June 1981. Parramore's manufactured iron castings on a site at the top end of Smith Street. Alex Parramore's grandfather started the firm in 1904. At the time of closure almost 200 were employed at the firm. Paramo Tools continued to trade.

Opposite below: Naylors' fish and rabbit shop in the early 1900s. This shop was one of a small group near Chapeltown railway bridge which was demolished to make way for the shops below Asda. Mrs Naylor sold wet fish and rabbits; her sister, Mrs Bennett, cooked fish and chips for the saloon. The shop sign, 'Direct from Grimsby', serves as a reminder of a family tragedy. The Naylor's eldest son, Lewis, used to travel to Sheffield on his motorbike at 4 a.m. each morning to meet the Grimsby train to collect the fish. Sadly, one morning he was killed, caught up between two tramcars.

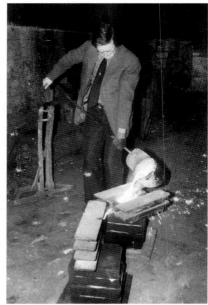

Opposite above: Chapeltown in the 1960s. The Yorkshire Bank is on the left and Chapeltown House in the centre. The shops on the right are Anita Mary Hattersley's hairdressers and a sweet shop.

Opposite below: Charlton Ironworks pictured in the late 1980s, just prior to closure. Charlton Brook Ironworks was listed in 1879 as a brass and iron foundry, established by Rebecca Ogden. By 1898–99, George Harvey had taken over the firm and was making cooking ranges and mantels among other things. By 1947 it had become Charlton Ironworks and, while still making cooking ranges, had begun to specialise in manhole covers and street gulley drain covers and frames.

Right: E.M. Senior's grocery shop and general store in Mount Road, Charlton Brook.

Below: The first coal lorry purchased by Walter Morris of Burncross. Joe Stead, one of the drivers, is standing on the right.

Above: Jack Barnes' garage, Hollow Gate. Initially it was a tyre shop and small garage, but an extension was built in 1960–61. Jack retired in 1982 though the garage still operates.

Left: George Arthur Marshall, gardener at Barnes Hall from 1922 to 1948.

Four

Teachers and Pupils

The Feoffees School in Ecclesfield stood on the corner of Priory Road as early as 1573, when there is a record of its repair. It continued on that site until 1854 when it moved into the altered Feoffees Hall. A second school, Rawson's Infants School, was built and endowed by Miss Hannah Rawson of Wardsend in 1834. Dr Gatty claimed that when he first came to the village in 1839 the master at the Feoffees School was insane and that Rawson's Infants School was run by an old woman who signed with a cross when he paid her quarterly salary. Things were no better at High Green at the beginning of the 1840s. Of a dame school there in 1841, the sub-commissioner for the Children's Employment Commission said 'to talk of education would be a mockery in such a place'. The other 'education' there was provided by an old cripple who was more famed for 'supernatural witchcraft touching missing bodies, stolen goods and stray pigs' than for his teaching abilities. In 1843, High Green School, on Wortley Road, was built with money raised by voluntary subscriptions and grants from the British and Foreign Society. In Chapeltown a school existed at the top of Lound, founded in 1716. At Grenoside there was an endowed school in School Lane from 1807 for poor children and a National School from 1876. Following the 1870 Education Act the quality of education was greatly improved and Board Schools were established at Burncross, Ecclesfield, Grenoside, Lound and Warren. The twentieth century has seen the further extension of educational opportunities including the opening in 1931 of Ecclesfield Grammar School.

Miss Marsden's class at Ecclesfield Junior School in the 1920s. Back row, from left to right: Evelyn Hartley, -?-, -?-, Doris Wells, Edith Kelsey, Sally Knott, Jack Aukland, Annie Jolly, Gladys Wallace, Willy Thomas, Tilly Hughes. Fourth row: Barbara Sorsby, Bessie Jubb, Sam Jarvis, Leonard Henderson, Albert Wilson, Lewis Fletcher, Florrie Fox, May Alison, Harry Gregory, ? Adcock, -?-, Miss Marsden. Third row: Edith Greaves, Doris Alen, Gwen Royal, Harold Sorsby, -?-, -?-, George Higgins, Stanley Hall, Alan Tims, -?-, Ralph Cutts, Linda Beard. Second row: -?-, Annie Wilmott, Lizzie Greaves, -?-, Ruth Milner, Betty Gregory, Maggie Cox, Irene Hayes, -?-, May Hartley, Herbert Maw. Front row: Jack Flather, Jack Wilmott, Jim Flather, Garnet Stringer, ? Greensmith, ? Crossland, Eric Waller, Irwin Wallace, Eric Rider Harold Jones.

Some of the staff at Ecclesfield Town Junior School. Back row, from left to right: Miss Lazarus, Miss Holland, Miss Sharp, Mrs Robinson. Front: Miss Weldon, Miss Marsden.

Ecclesfield Grammar School, hockey team, 1940s. Back row, from left to right: Mr Harrison (headteacher), Gwen Fisher, Jean Denton, Sheila Fallon or Joyce Price, Joanna Connell, Maureen Smith, Margaret Robertson, Miss Henry (PE teacher). Front row: Irene Wilkinson, Betty Smithies, Marie Donald, Jean Baldwin, Ann Falk.

Ecclesfield Grammar School, Form VA, 1956. Back row, from left to right: David Heath, Peter Bacon, Frank Pickering, Eric Hall, Anthony Kent, Leslie Grant, Howard Moxon, Graham Perry, David Bottomley, Michael Mumford. Middle row: Norma Peace, Barbara Manley, Anthea Cutts, June Siddall, Dennis Smith, Duncan Heney, Pamela Lowe, Juliet Helliwell, Christine Parker, June Matthews. Front row: Beryl Davison, Valerie Catcliffe, Judy Emerson, Lois Barraclough, Cynthia Foster, Mr Wessley (French teacher), Margaret Childs, Margaret Ward, Eileen Anderson, Pat Wild, Anita Marsh. Ann Perry was absent on the day of the photograph.

This certificate was presented to Myra Beever on 13 July 1887 for successfully passing the annual examination at the end of Standard Two. She attended Grenoside National School and was examined by HM Inspector, E.H. Howard. The certificate is also signed by the master, F. Shaw.

Grenoside Board School, infant class, in 1901. Willis Gibson, of Barnes Green Farm, can be seen fourth from the right on the front row. The children are wearing their Sunday best on this special weekday occasion.

Alice Keene, the Grenoside May Queen, in 1911 with her attendants. As was the custom, May flowers are present in profusion, in baskets around the queen's feet and in the form of garlands in her female attendants' hair. Miss Turner, the headteacher of the infant school, revived the old May Day custom of having a May Day queen.

Grenoside Infant School, Rose Day celebrations in the school yard in 1949. Margaret Johnson is the Rose Queen.

Grenoside Infant School continue with their Rose Day festivities by dancing round the maypole. Mrs Brook, one of the staff, can be seen encouraging and instructing.

High Green Secondary Modern School staff, 1948. This is the first photograph of staff following the amalgamation of Lound Girls' School and High Green Boys' School. Back row, from left to right: -?- (student teacher), H. Fullelove, C.B. Rudkin, A. Eyre, J. Greenwood, D. Hughes, Mr Johnson, A. Gledhill. Front row: Miss Hartley, Joan Gradwell, E. Williams, Mr F. Piper (headteacher), Mrs Staines, F. Trickett, C. Bennett.

High Green Secondary Modern School, Wharncliffe House cricket team, 1950. Back row, from left to right: Martin Rollings, Derek Watkinson, Frank Martin, Roy Whittington, George Beever, Brian Hulbert. Front row: Trevor Barrass, Geoff Smith, Keith Oxborough, Billy Locking, Alwyn Belcher.

High Green Infants School, coronation celebrations, 1953.

High Green Infants presented their version of the Westminster Abbey coronation to a large crowd of parents and friends. The boys opened the ceremony dressed as soldiers, complete with drummers. The procession included Glenn Rooker as the Archbishop of Canterbury, Alan Pickering as the Lord Chamberlain, Michael Lofts as the Duke of Edinburgh and Kathryn Ellis as Queen Elizabeth.

Burncross Primary School, a class from the 1920s. Back row, from left to right: Eva Harvey, E. Elliott, Ivy Brooks, Rose Colton, ? Richards, A. Goddard, A. Evans, B. Padley, N. Locking. Fourth row: Mr Platts (headteacher), Freda Dearden, Bob Lax, S. Williamson, F. Brooks, Irene Shaw, Cyril Bywater, A. Howel or ? Hague, Mr Bramwell. Third row: N. Hattersley, B. Beighton, ? Hague, Mary Mellor, -?-, -?-, Fred Hurst, Lena Shaw. Second row: Ruth Barrow, Cyril Butcher, ? Foweather, ? Hill, Muriel Barlow, Cyril Laycock, B. Saxton, Bob Cole, Reg Rudd. Front row: Charlie Pearson, Sarah Smith, Cyril Dransfield, Trissy Warburton.

Burncross Primary School, 1931. Those pictured are the pupils who passed the examination to go to Ecclesfield Grammar School with Mr Platts (front row, centre). Back row, from left to right: Douglas Barnes, Harold Kay, Frank Barrow, Joe Marshall, Billy Platts, Jack Birks, Gordon Bellamy, Donald Hudson, Will Rawlin. Front row: Marian Barraclough, Audrey Copley, Olga Arthur, Edith George, Hilda Bellamy, Jean Rice, Kathleen Thorne, Mary Donald.

Burncross Infants, a class in 1959, with Mrs Tantum. Back row, from left to right: Robert Hutchinson, Rory Gregory, Elizabeth Mayfield, Ann Muir, Sandra Stead, Stephen Kay, Linda Moxon, Denise Cooke. Middle row: Brenda Shaw, Linda Sidebottom, Helen Stewart, Rosemary Jezusek, May Maw, Susan Myers, Richard Goddard, Margaret Burgin. Front row: Veronica Whittaker, Graham Taylor, Jacqueline Parkin, Robert Greaves, Derek ?, Stephen French, Eric Dexter, Jean Gregory, Stephen Armitage.

Burncross Junior School football team in 1966 with Mr B. Kirbyshaw. Back row, from left to right: David Steel, Andrew Howell, Andrew Lax, Robin Slater, Stuart Whitman, Anthony Dawson, Philip Ackroyd. Front row: Gary Newbould, Clive Gregory, Kevin Redfearn, Andrew Kay, Adrian Midgley.

Five

Parades, Carnivals and Gatherings

The cultural life of the area covered by Ecclesfield, Grenoside, High Green and Chapeltown has always been remarkably rich and varied. It ranges from the family with its seasonal gatherings and visits, to the informal cultural life of the street which comes together on special occasions such as coronations and military victories, to formal organisations such as the church, chapel, Scouts and Guides, the operatic society, brass band and sports clubs. Newton Chambers, the largest employer in the area for over a century and a half, also had a profound effect on the development of certain cultural, sporting and leisure time activities. Some traditional events – such as the Grenoside Sword Dancers on Boxing Day, the Ecclesfield Beagles and the local carolling tradition – have made the villages well known in the wider region. Some of the most well attended occasions were money-raising events such as the hospital parades which were such a colourful feature of the area in the half century before the Second World War.

Ecclesfield Grammar School party. They stayed in a youth hostel on the Isle of Arran in 1947 – one of many trips organised by Mr Dick Endall.

Harvest Festival in the 'Upper Room' Sunday school, Butterthwaite. This room was a small loft over a cowshed with an outside stairway. It was repaired and cleaned by the residents at Butterthwaite and used for many years as a Sunday school, for meetings, plays and whist drives.

Anthea Cutts, 'Lily of the Valley' Queen. For many years Ecclesfield Girl Guides held May celebrations when their queen was crowned. The Guide leaders were Miss Ivy Phillips (the local post-mistress) and Miss Violet Jefferies.

Part of the May Queen celebrations by Ecclesfield Girl Guides on the vicarage lawn, *c.* 1947. Margot Hirst leads the guardsmen under the arch.

The golden wedding celebrations of Richard and Sarah Ridge of Ecclesfield, in 1950. The party was held in the school room of Trinity Methodist chapel (now the Eppic Theatre building) and many friends and relations attended. Those present included Joyce Day, Nancy Brookes, Mr Hallam, Frank Moxon, Nellie Brookes, Mary Brookes, Joan Wallace, Margaret Bentley, Mr Hodges, Betty Greaves, Albert Renshaw, Eileen Cooper, Barbara Ridge, Mr and Mrs Flather, Derrick Roe, Albert Flather, Ron Baxter, Mrs Rodgers, Alf Day, Peter Leaske, Frank Fletcher, Fred Brookes, Jennifer Brookes, Herbert Purdy, Paul Brookes, Albert Ibbotson, Jack Garrison, Atkin Clayton, Daisy Renshaw, Elsie Baxter, Alice Armitage, Kathleen Ibbotson, Audrey Hodges, Kate Hodges, Lily Dawson, Ellis Purdy, Lily Purdy, Colin Dawson, Edith Clayton, Norma Leaske, Rene Hutchinson, Frank Whitaker, Kathleen Moxon, Hilary Moxon, Ida Fletcher, Marie Renshaw, Christine Day, Christine Ibbotson, Malcolm Ridge, Gillian Ridge, Glyn Baxter, Mrs Houghton and Anthea Cutts.

Ecclesfield Hospital Parade-1906

Ecclesfield Hospital Parade, in 1906. This took place on the Common, Ecclesfield. In the days before the National Health Service was introduced, hospitals depended for much of the money they needed on bequests, endowments and public generosity. Hospital parades were started, in Ecclesfield, Grenoside and High Green, to collect for this good cause. They were held from the early 1890s until about 1936. Neighbours would get together and decorate a cart in secret. A metal or wood-worker would make a frame which was then cleverly covered with coloured paper. Local farmers lent their horses to pull the carts. The horses were decorated with freshly-polished brasses. Mary and Albert Salt of Ecclesfield remember the Ecclesfield Parade which started on the Saturday afternoon of the third weekend after Whitsuntide. The decorated carts were first taken to Station Road to be judged and then the parade would set off. Collectors walked beside the carts to gather pennies from the crowds that lined the route. The parade went along Ecclesfield Common, up Church Street to Grenoside, down to Wadsley Bridge, past the Infirmary and across to the bottom of The Moor, up The Moor, along High Street to the Wicker, up to Firth Park, Bellhouse Road, Shiregreen, Hatfield House Lane, down Barnsley Road and back to Stocks Hill. By this time it would be almost 8.00p.m. and those with any energy left went to the Feast beside the Ball Inn. On Sunday afternoon, there was a sing in Bank House Gardens and then, on Monday evening, the parade re-assembled. It proceeded up the hill to Chapeltown, up Burncross and along to the Crown Inn, turned off to the Rose Inn, down Wortley Road in High Green to Lane End and turned on to Sussex Road, usually ending up at Chapeltown Feast. What a weekend!

Part of Ecclesfield Hospital Parade is pictured outside Creasers' blacksmiths shop. This was situated next to the Travellers Inn at the southern end of the Common.

Ecclesfield Hospital Parade in 1909. They proceed along the Common, approaching the junction with Mill Lane and Nether Lane.

Spectators watching the Ecclesfield Hospital Parade from the height of the churchyard as the parade comes up Church Street on its route to Grenoside.

The 'Plough Bullocks', 1908. A favourite part of the Ecclesfield Hospital Parade was the Plough Bullocks. A plough was put onto a low cart or trolley which was then pulled by a team of 'ploughmen', all wearing countrymen's smocks. They were driven by a man in similar attire who smote them heartily with a blown-up pig's bladder fastened to a stick. It was very thirsty work so frequent stops were made at welcoming hostelries where the 'bullocks' quaffed their ale from a bucket.

Grenoside Hospital Parade, in 1909, outside the Primitive Methodist chapel schoolroom on Main Street.

Whitsuntide walk from St Mark's church, Grenoside. Church members and scholars are on their way to the sing in Grenoside Park in 1963. Peter Bradshaw is carrying the cross.

Henry Mollart, of Grenoside, knur and spell champion. The object of this game was to hit the knur, or ball, as far as possible. The knur weighed about 2oz and was made of either wood or pot. The knur was placed in a shallow cup (the spell) which was attached to a spring held in place by a trigger, which was released by tapping it with the hitting stick sometimes called a pummel or driver. This was approximately six feet long with a special head measuring about 4 inches by 3 inches. Considerable skill was needed to give that precise tap so that the ball reached the required height for hitting forcefully. Knur and spell matches attracted large crowds and heavy betting.

Despite the steep slopes, cycling has always been a popular pastime in the area. In this case the group is thought to be quarrymen, from Beever's Quarry, Grenoside, sometime before the First World War.

Snow house, Grenoside, 1893. The snow house was constructed at Skew Hill, Grenoside, in January 1893, when there was a great snow and frost and the quarrymen were frozen out for sixteen weeks. Well-trodden snow was piled in a heap about 24 feet long, 14 feet wide and 10 feet high and left for 48 hours. A room 18 feet long, 8 feet wide and 6 feet high was cut at the south end and a chimney placed at the north end. A table was put at the centre of the room and around it 50 outdoor workers and their wives took tea, donated by Mr T. Machen. After tea there was entertainment consisting of songs by Joseph Steel, A.J. Westerman, R. Stringer, Joe Machen, G. Hawksworth, W. Denton, F. Housley, J.H. Burkinshaw and Joe Fleetwood and recitations by Mr C. Ryder. There was also dancing with Mr Joshua Fleetwood as the accompanist. The next evening 20 people had supper and games and the following night the youngsters were entertained. On these fine, moonlit nights hundreds of villagers visited the snow house, a local wonder!

Opposite above: A further view of the snow house in 1893.

Opposite below: Milk is being delivered on School Lane by Mr Beal, of Hallfield Head, during the great snow of February 1947. For nearly two months, snow clearing became a community activity. Mr Beal cleared the Woodhead Road into Grenoside in order to deliver milk. He hitched a sled behind one of his horses to carry the churns from which he dispensed measured jugs of milk.

Grenoside Sword Dancers. No one seems to know when the sword dance started in Grenoside or what its origins are. The basis may lie in distant times when a man or an animal was slaughtered by a tribe as a sacrifice to propitiate the gods. Early in the dance the lock (seen above), made of interlaced swords, is placed around the kneeling captain's neck. After a slow dance around him, the lock is suddenly disentangled by the team, the swords drawn across his neck and the captain's helmet falls symbolically to the ground. The onlookers witness what is perhaps an echo of a primitive religion, a mock sacrifice. In the nineteenth century and up to the Second World War the dance was performed annually on Christmas Eve and Boxing Day in the village streets, on stone-flagged floors in inns and in the big houses in the parish. Now the dancers perform on Boxing Day in Grenoside and all the year through at festivals. They dance to tunes played on a fiddle.

St Mark's church, Grenoside, enjoy their annual outing to the coast in 1950. Revd Heppenstall stands towards the right.

Grenoside church choir on an outing to Southport, in June 1952.

Lord Rowallan opening Grenoside Scout headquarters in 1948. This has now been replaced by a new building.

Grenoside Cub pack in Hesley Wood, Chapeltown in 1961. Thousands of Scouts and Cubs have benefitted from the provision of the outdoor activity centre in Hesley Wood.

Whit Sing, at Whitley Hall, in the early 1900s. Scholars and members of the Methodist chapels of Grenoside used to parade to Whitley Hall with their banners for the annual Whit Sing.

The fishing team of the Cart and Horses, High Green, 1936–37, with their trophies. The men fished in the local dams and made excursions into Lincolnshire. Back row, from left to right: Fred Matthewman, Mr Winterbottom, Arthur Lakin, Frank Fisher, Ellis Matthewman. Front row: Wilf Clark, Joseph Jackson, Mr Rawson.

High Green Hospital Parade float *c.* 1938. Mrs Evelyn Fox, Mrs Denton (at the tub), Mrs Westnedge and Mrs Ellis take part in the fund-raising event.

British Legion Parade, Ladies Section, High Green. The flag party consists of Mrs Denton, Mrs Fox and Mrs Jordan. Harold West can be seen on the rostrum holding his walking stick. Standing near the wall are Father Reynolds, Dr Gault and Mr Denton.

High Green Scouts, 1953, with their Scoutmaster, Eric Gale (extreme left). These Scouts were all awarded their First Class Badges, a unique event in the Wentworth Association. Back row, from left to right: Tony Wright, Geoff Millward, Dennis Smith, Tony Cooke. Front row: Geoff Simpson, John Vickers, David Crisp, Jack Bassinder, Robert Parkin, Michael Cooper.

Potter Hill chapel outing.

Whitsuntide parade along Mortomley Lane in 1960. In the foreground the banner of Stoneygate Primitive Methodist chapel is being carried.

Mortomley St Saviour's church outing to Bridlington, 1950s. Included in the group are Ernest Housley, John Kaye, Mr and Mrs Norman, Cliff, Alice, Patsy, Brian and John Davis, Percy Sansam, Mr and Mrs Johnson, Mr Kilner, Arthur, Philip and Laura Sansam, the Mellor family, Robert Wombwell, Alan Higgins and John Greenwood.

Mortomley St Saviour's Mothers' Union tea, c. 1955. From left to right: Mrs Alice Davis, Mrs Mellor, Mrs Whitfield, Mrs Wombwell.

St Saviour's Nativity, 1950. Those taking part included John Greenwood, Arthur Sansam, John Kaye, David Mellor, Philip Sansam, Mr Kilner, Graham Johnson, Brian Davis, Martin Taylor, John Davis, Maisie Vero and Betty Marshall.

Mortomley Cricket Club dance in the Miners' Welfare Hall, High Green, early 1950s. Back row, from left to right: John Kaye, Michael Smith, Graham Bennett. Front row: Maisie Vero, Muriel Robinson, Mavis Maskell, Betty Marshall, Pat Lindley, Joyce Yeardley.

Coronation tea, at the Miners' Welfare Hall, High Green, in 1953. All those who lived on Vickers Road had been paying 6d a week to fund the celebrations.

Coronation celebrations at the crossroads in High Green, 1953. Among those present were Tom Ashton, the Kenworthys, Willis Andrews, Mrs Andrews, Alice Brailsford, Mrs Woodward, Ian Rose, June Wright, Mr and Mrs Wheeler, Ann Simpson, Mrs Burtoft and Mary Burtoft.

Daniel Chappell Dransfield (left) with his sisters, Grace (centre) and Lily (right) c. 1915. Their parents were Daniel and Priscilla Dransfield of High Green. The trio were noted musicians who regularly gave concerts in the district. Grace taught at High Green School on Wortley Road and often conducted the Whit Sing on Mortomley Hill.

American soldiers baptise a group in Howbrook Dam during the Second World War. At this time American soldiers were stationed at Potter Hill camp.

Thorncliffe Ironworks, Heavy Castings Department, drawing office staff, at their Christmas party in 1950. Among the families and friends are Chris Harrison, Graham Cawthorn, Bob Taylor, Jean Deakin, Margaret Bellamy, Bruce Cadwallender, Mabel Rollin, Joan Atherton and Mrs Dexter.

Festival of Britain celebrations in 1951 organised by Newton Chambers. Crowds cheer the races.

The second annual dinner of Thorncliffe Foreman's Association, in December 1959. The event was held at the Marquis of Granby in Bamford. From left to right: Mr C. Pease, Mr H. Lewis, Mrs C. Taylor, Mrs C. Pease, Mr F. Whitehouse, Mrs H. Lewis, Mr C. Taylor, Mrs G. Bywater, Mr P.J.C. Bovill, Mrs B. Gale, Mrs P.J.C. Bovill, Mrs L. Godber, Mr C.V. Bywater, Mr B. Gale, Mr L. Godber, Mrs R.S. Goodhind, Mrs F. Whitehouse, Mr R.S. Goodhind.

Scholars and friends of Burncross Methodist chapel return from the Whit Sing in Chapeltown Park, *c.* 1957. The Sunday school queen is Myra Marsden, pictured with her attendant, Roger Ackroyd. Wendy Brown (right) holds a rope of the banner. Eric Oliver carries one pole (on the left) and Ian Hodgkin can be seen behind Eric with another rope.

The Sunday school queens at Burncross Methodist chapel began their year of office when they were crowned at the Harvest Festival service on the first Sunday in October, in this case in the late 1950s. From left to right: June Cooper, Valerie Downend (retiring queen), Paul Burrows, Richard Goddard, Jean Gregory, Susan Greaves.

Sunday school queens, attendants and captains at Station Road Methodist chapel, in Chapeltown in the early 1960s. Back row, from left to right: Sheila Rodgers, Julie Wharam, Clive Bailey, Christine Brooke, Alan Ashton, David Winkley, Christine Trickett. Middle row: Maria Mucha, Judith Elliot, Jacqueline Rodgers, Janet Crossland, Sandra Lakin, -?-. Front row boys: Ian Burkinshaw (left) and John Smith (right).

Sunday school queen and attendants, at Warren Methodist chapel. From left to right: Stuart Collins, Rita Trickett, Margaret Smith, Marjorie Thompson, Betty Johnson, Lily Hague, Ann Wildman, Nancy Needham, Malcolm Smith. Marlene Davis is at the front.

A performance of *Aladdin* at the Newton Hall in 1946. Included in the cast are Jean Portman, Charlie Hague, Bessie Gale, Betty Hitchman, Tom Marsh, Pat Seale and Joan Turner.

Wedding at Greenhead Mount Zion Wesleyan Reform chapel in the early 1900s. The bridegroom was Fred Fullelove who lived in one of the cottages behind Mount Pleasant chapel and his bride was Annie Wilson of Normanton. Among the relations present was Sarah Cliffe (née Johnson), far left, carrying her son, Jim, and hoping to hide her cheek swollen with toothache. Next to her is Pleasance Wilson who married Ernest Trickett (who rests his hands on her shoulders). Behind Ernest is William Cliffe of Cowley Lane, Chapeltown.

Chapel anniversary at Warren, in 1936. Included among the members (roughly from the back) are Harold Platts, Billy Hill, Nelly Armitage, Joyce Parkin, Sheila Lee, Edith Bowyer, Betty Kilner, Eva Lambert, Elsie Wilkinson, Rene Clarke, Olive Smart, Mary Pepper, Annie Newbold, Nelly Bassinder, Gladys Stutchbury, Gladys Marshall, Maisy Bond, Connie Newbold, Mrs Fisher, Grace Stutchbury, Mrs Chapman, Harry Renshaw, Harry Evans, Hilda Mellor, Mrs Crooks, Mary Giles, Emma Moxon, Mrs Hoyland, May Galloway, Mrs Galloway, Isaac Hill, Fred Lambert and Mr Jackson.

This group poses outside the Royal Oak, Chapeltown. They are all dressed to the nines.

Outing to Doncaster races from the New Inn, Bracken Hill. James Morris is at the reins and Charles and Arthur Marsden sit on either side of him.

The Willis first aid competition, in 1958, was held at the Miners' Welfare Hall, Chapeltown. Back row, from left to right: Reg Hobson, Cyril Dransfield, Terry Bintcliffe, Graham Chambers, Albert Schofield, George Ingram. Middle row: Joe Derrin, William Fox, Wilfred Goddard, Tom Frost, Harry Hartley. Front row: Edmund Ellis, Garnet North, Richard Hartley, Albert Chappel, Jim Gallant, Harvey Sidebottom.

Silver Jubilee celebrations, Hall Wood Road, Bracken Hill, in 1977. The 'Queen of Rotherham Road' (now Hallwood Road) was Tamara Whitham. She was crowned by Dorothy Willett and can be seen, with her attendants, Kay Hitchmough, Dennie Hall, Claire Bassinder and Craig Taylor, on her regal tour of Bracken Hill. She was driven by Mick Womersley in his horse and trap.

Possibly a Burncross chapel outing. On the back row, third from the left, is Harry Haslam; in the middle is Harry Edwards with Felix Womersley second from the right. Kneeling on the left is Charlie Rudkin with Gladys Rudkin in front of him and Annie Womersley in front of her. Evelyn Edwards is fourth from the left (wearing a long necklace); immediately on the right is Percy Crossland and Mrs Ruby Haslam is third from the right at the front.

A group of ladies at Burncross Methodist chapel. Mrs Shotton stands at the back on the left and Mrs Timmons is on the right. In the middle row Mrs Saunders is on the left and Mrs Nicholson is third from the right.

A concert held at Burncross chapel during the First World War to raise money to buy 'comforts' for the troops.

Comforts for the troops in the First World War. These were bought with money raised in Burncross, Bracken Hill and Charlton Brook.

Chapeltown Scouts at Folkestone, c. 1948. Back row, from left to right: G. Marshall, D. Mason, R. Edwards, E. Eyre, A. Hague, H. Winterbottom, A. Goulding, H. Smith, A. Haines, K. Price, P. Hitchmough. Middle row: ? Holt, R. Luckett, T. Purvis, N. Wilkinson, G. Beaver, J. Charlesworth, I. Luckett, -?-. Front row: ? Williams, A. Taylor, G. Hitchmough, G. Hines, G. Simpson, B. Charlesworth, T. Luckett, ? Luckett, ? Luckett, N. Lee.

Mount Pleasant Methodist chapel flower festival. Mr J. Parramore is presented with a bunch of carnations. Harry Haslam is looking down on the right (wearing glasses).

Terry Wilkinson, John Ogle and John Fullelove practise on their tenor horns in the Midland Hotel (now The Escape) for Chapeltown Silver Prize Band in the 1960s. In 1975 band members transformed the old Station Road Methodist chapel into a practice room for the band.

The wedding of Lawrence and Dorothy Perry in 1921. On the front row, from left to right: Mrs Turner, Edith Winter, John Winter, Rene Binder, Mary Tricket, Lawrence and Dorothy Perry, Aubrey Horrocks, Mary Fisher, Gwen Binder, Mrs Binder, Betty Horrocks, Mr Binder. Other local families present included the Boltons, Stuarts, Carrs, Badgers and Garners.

An Edwardian wedding possibly at Chapeltown. The men are resplendent in top hats, bowlers and even a straw boater, tailcoats, waistcoats with watch chains, white bow ties, stiff collars and large button holes. The ladies are in their Edwardian best, topped by magnificent hats. Behind them, on the wall, local children have climbed up to see what all the hullabaloo is about. Two of the guests present are Jonathan (Jonty) Greaves and his wife Sally, pictured on the extreme right of the middle row. The value of this superb photograph is lessened because of lack of information. We would urge all our readers to gather as much detail as possible about the old (and new!) photographs in their possession – before they forget and before those who could tell them are no longer able to do so!

Another two carefully posed portraits shot 'on location' in the local countryside. These were in the form of glass negatives stored for many years in a garage, but sadly no one has been able to identify the subjects.

Supporters at the Chapeltown & High Green Archive tenth anniversary exhibition at the Newton Hall, Chapeltown, in October 1997.

Acknowledgements

The authors would like to thank the following for the donation or loan of photographs and/or accompanying information:

Philip Ackroyd, Bert Almond, Myra Barley, Marian Barraclough, Edith Barton, Charlie Bassinder, Margaret Batson, Joan Batten, Beryl Beever, Ted Bellamy, Molly Birtcliffe, Terry Birtcliffe, the late Alan Boulton, Charles Boyes, Connie Boyes, Shirley Bramald, Jean Brown, Gwen Bywater, Grace Cauwood, Chris and Peter Chapman, the late Annie Cavill, the late Bill Childs, Mary Clarke, Jessie Cole, Alan Copley, Elsie Cotton, David Crisp, John Davis, Bryan Dawson, David Dickinson, Trissy Dransfield, Raymond and Margaret Edwards, the late George Elliot, Jean Ellis, Jim Ellis, Gwen Elmhirst, June Falding, Doris Faries, Bessie Flather, Ted Frost, Brian Gale, Betty Galloway, Jeff Galloway, Ada Gibson, the late Daisy Gibson, Julie Goddard, Joan Gradwell, Anthea Greaves, Beryl Greaves, Frank Greaves, the late Gladys Greaves, John Greaves, Trevor Greaves, Clive Gregory, Grenoside Local History Group, Grenoside Scouts, Roy Hartley, the late Edwin Hobson, Jessie Hobson, Alan Jackson, Evelyn Jenkinson, Amy Jones, Joseph ine and Charlie Jordan, Ray Kay, Norman Kirk, Shirley Kirk, Gillian Lacey, Peter Leask, Jean and Norman Lewis, Joan Lockwood, Melvyn Lodge, the late Florence Marshall, Heather Marshall, Wilf Marshall, Frank Martin, Ivan Martin, Jean Mellor Chris and Pat Morley, Pat and William Morton, Newton Chambers and Co., John Ogle Ernest Parramore, Derek Renshaw, Norma Rice, Frank Rodgers, Albert and Mary Salt, Brian Senior, Beryl Shaw, George Sheldon, Albert Shelton, Cyril Slinn, Doreen and Len Smith the late Sydney Smith, R. Stansfield, the late Ron Thomas, Bill Timms, Nora Turp, Margo Tye, Bryan Wadsworth, Edward Watkinson, Jill Whitham, Eric Wilson, Marjorie and Neville Wilkinson, Jacqueline Winkley, Leslie Womersley, Mick and Sheila Womersley, Eve Woods Glenys Wraith and Winnie Yeardley.

The map of the district was drawn by Bob Warburton.

We apologise if we have inadvertently omitted the name of any contributor.